Fathers

The world's first gender equality
catalogue for children and fathers

Jesper Lohse

Author: Jesper Lohse
Published by Amazon.

World Parents Organization
Registered socio-economic organization (RSV)
E-mail: info@worldparents.org
Website: worldparents.org
Cvr. 28699727

Publication: 1st edition 2021
ISBN: 9798711960522

Preface

The world's first gender equality catalog for children and fathers has been created using Denmark as the case. The catalog includes 12 themes and 366 topics based on several years of analysis of family situations and family law.

The catalog has been created as inspiration and documentation for international policy makers, researchers, media, citizens, human rights institutions, and courts.

Many countries have legal obligation under articles 2, 3 and 7 of the UN Convention on the Rights of the Child and articles 6, 8, 14 and 17 of the European Convention on Human Rights.

It is a human right for children to know and be cared for by their parents. It is a human right to gain respect for family life and it is a human right to be protected against discrimination.

We must ask ourselves the question. Does this apply for children, fathers, grandparents, and shared parenting families in modern society?

Discrimination in society of almost half of the population must be rectified.

This is the responsibility of policy makers, national parliaments, and every public leader. As well as international institutions such as the United Nations, Council of Europe, European Commission and human rights and gender equality protection agencies.

We face a new reality related to children and fathers in modern society. It might be here we find the greatest potential for success related to personal freedom, equal opportunities, public health, public savings, and increased quality of life.

It might be here we find the future welfare model of every society.

This book looks at new opportunities and challenges in modern family life and the society.

Yours sincerely,
Jesper Lohse

Table of contents

Positive father involvement

Every society should ensure equal opportunities for women and men in both work and family life.

This is healthy for society and for the children. It is the welfare model of the future and will create a success in any country.

Why is positive father involvement important!

- Positive father involvement creates personal freedom and equal opportunities for women and men, boys, and girls in society.

- Positive father involvement creates more healthy children in society with a good and loving upbringing, clear identity, and improved mental health.

- Positive father involvement prevents life crises and conflicts. It creates less stressed family life, in society.

- Positive father involvement creates fewer vulnerable children and citizens – and therefore less social spending.

- Positive father involvement creates more trust, security, and love in family life for everyone.

It is all about personal freedom, equal opportunities, public health, and respect of people.

New family law

The future family law is based on love and equality as a basic assumption for ordinary citizens as well as good quality for the children and parents who need society's help.

We shall keep it simple and make a modern family legislation that work today. Legislation that complies with the UN Convention on the Rights of the Child and the European Human Right Convention. This is possible.

The basic principle:

Level A
All children have an equal right to the father and mother as the basic assumption.

Level B
All parents have a free choice to make their own agreements between them.

Level C
A family court with children experts can make court decisions on concerns for children based on parental behavior.

For these principles, the following 10 recommendations can be used to create a new family law.

10 recommendations

§1 The child's parents are the biological father and mother in respect of other caregivers who give the child love, care, and security in life. Children have a human right to know and be cared for by their parents.

§2 The child's parents must have the same public information.

§3 The child has the right to equal parental leave with each parent.

§4 All parents have joint custody by law, unless special circumstances count against it

§5 If the parents do not live together, the child has living residence with both parents and equal parenting time 50% / 50% as the basic assumption.

§6 The child's financial income and expenses are distributed 50% / 50% between the parents at equal or largely equal parenting time. In the case of weekend visitation or less, one parent secures the child's finances against a normal child allowance based on both parent's income and ability to work.

§7 If a parent moves more than 80 km / 1 hour away, the moving parent handles the transport of the child as the basic assumption.

§8 The parents have the freedom to make another agreement if desired in the best interest of the child.

§9 If there is concern for the child by a parent or authority, the case is dealt with by a family court. A certified assistant can be involved for the child.

§10 A family court can, for compelling reasons, make another decision with a focus on gender equality, documentation and in the best interests of the child. All allegations of criminal conduct are processed by the police.

Theme 1: Parenthood

Few citizens in Denmark are aware that, in accordance with the children's act, the child's parents are not registered as the biological father and mother as the basic assumption. It is the biological mother or husband. The biological father is not mentioned in the legislation.

The Children's Act was made in the early 1900s but is still used today in a time with shared parenting, DNA, cohabitation termination and social media, where biological children, parents and siblings find each other.

The only way we can protect children in the future, in an open world with full information is however, with the truth, equal opportunities, and the reward of good values and behavior.

Most people have great respect for two women or two men that love each other and want to live together in addition to single parents who want to have children.

The important thing is that we have respect for people and diversity but also have respect for biological parenting, which is lifelong emotional as it is the origin of the child. Children must never become toys in the adults' sandbox.

All children have a human right to know and be cared for by their parents.

The following things should be noted:

1. The child's father is in principle the husband and not necessarily the child's biological father in the legislation.

2. Fathers are not always notified of biological parenthood, whereby the child may have an incorrect father registered.

3. The employer has the right to notified of the child before the biological father.

4. The child has no right to have both parents' names.

5. Children must have the biological parenthood determined within 6 months, even if mistakes occur and the truth is not told.

6. Children may have incorrect registration of biological parenthood despite DNA technology.

7. Children may have incorrect registration of biological parenthood despite termination of cohabitation.

8. Children may have incorrect registration of biological parenthood despite social media where children, parents, siblings, and other family members find each other today.

9. Children may have incorrect registration of biological parenthood despite new image recognition technology that can find relatives globally.

10. Children may have incorrect registration of biological parenting despite Mobile Apps which can match and find all information for a person you meet on the street or in a cafe.

11. Fathers do not have automatic custody as a biological father.

12. Fathers do not necessarily have custody because it only became normal after 2007.

13. Fathers most often experience loss of custody, even if they are not the cause due to another parent's lack of cooperation and parental alienation.

14. Fathers must pay inheritance even if they become aware of incorrect registration of biological parenthood.

15. Fathers must pay child support even if there is incorrect registration of biological parenthood.

16. Anonymous sperm donation causes children to live in uncertainty about their biological origins.

17. Anonymous sperm donation means that children and parents cannot have biological parenthood recognized later in life, even if they change their mind because biological parenthood is emotionally lifelong.
18. Anonymous sperm donation prevents children and parents from finding a donor in a biological family.

19. A co-mother has in some countries the same rights as a biological father. Is this a violation of children right's?

20. Co-mother is included without co-father in the legislation, e.g., two men who want to have a child with a surrogate mother.

21. Fathers do not always want an abortion but do not have a choice.

22. Fathers do not always want the child but do not have a choice.

23. Children can be adopted against the fathers' will based on sole custody, even if parents do not have to have or may lose custody without it being their own fault.

24. Children can be adopted without the possibility of raising the case again.

25. Fathers do not always acknowledge biological parenthood.

26. Fathers do not always take responsibility for biological parenthood.

Theme 2: Public information

In connection with public information using digital mail, there is a simple explanation for why the mail is not sent to both parents. It is not possible to make a list of all children under the age of 18 in relation to custody and the right to information.

This is because data for both parents are missing in central registries. There can therefore be no automation of public information about children to both parents, despite the parents' right to equal information.

The consequence is a lack of citizen satisfaction and respect as well as large costs in manual workflows in schools, municipalities, hospitals and for the state. In addition, there is a loss of knowledge and far more human errors.

When examining the area for several years, it has seemed as if no officials want to take responsibility and inform the politicians clearly and distinctly. At the same time, it may be due to lobbying interests, but data is the core issue for the lack of public information to both parents.

The following things should be noted:

27. Public letters at the birth of the child are not sent automatically to both parents.

28. Public letters at maternity leave are not sent automatically to both parents.

29. Public letters at day care are not sent automatically to both parents.

30. Public letters at school enrollment are not sent automatically to both parents.

31. Public letters regarding. start and stop of institution is not sent automatically to both parents.

32. Public letters regarding start and stop of after-school programs are not automatically sent to both parents.

33. Public letters at the hospital are not sent automatically to both parents.

34. Public letters about health and satisfaction surveys are not automatically sent to both parents.

35. Public letters for family research are not automatically sent to both parents.

36. Public letters about education are not sent automatically to both parents.

37. Public letters at dental care are not sent automatically to both parents.

38. Public letters about leisure activities are not sent automatically to both parents.

39. Public letters of concern for children are not automatically sent to both parents.

40. Public hospital letters are not sent automatically to both parents due to manual procedures.

41. Public letters in municipalities and hospitals are not automatically sent to both parents due to human error.

42. Public letters in municipalities and hospitals are not automatically sent to both parents due to culture.

43. Public letters in municipalities and hospitals are not sent automatically to both parents due to unwillingness.

44. Parents, even if they have joint legal custody, may not always be notified of the child's doctor.

45. Parents may, even if they are not the cause, be without joint custody and may not have access to documents.

46. Parents are not always given everything by access to documents and do not always know what they are not given.

47. It will be possible to generate a timeline easily and automatically in public child and family cases for citizens. This by simple use of 'yyyy-mm-dd' before the title of documents

Theme 3: Paternal leave

When long parental leave was introduced in Denmark, the intention was for the child to experience leave with both parents for love, care, and security in life with both parents.

This has not happened in Denmark as the case because no earmarked leave period was set aside for fathers as in the rest of the Nordic region. Denmark is therefore significantly behind in relation to father's leave.

It is not correct when politicians and officials state that parents have a free choice. Children and fathers do not have it today.

The executive order on parental leave for example state, that if the parents disagree, the father and child are without rights, as the parental leave benefits are allocated to the parent where the child stays the most. In addition, very few ordinary fathers stand by the cradle and start arguing about the leave period and their little newborn child.

The children who need their father's leave the most are also often the children who do not get it e.g., in case of postpartum depression or negative social inheritance in the mother, where the father is kept away from the child. It may be the largest or one of the largest and most ignored groups of children with negative social heritage and mental health problems in society. It costs children and society dearly every year.

In addition, the Parental Responsibility Act says nothing about leave, which is why the father and child are effectively without rights if the parents do not live together or the cohabitation ends during the parental leave period. Few parents are aware that the leave can be used until the child reaches the age of 9, that the family law trumps the parental leave law if the parents do not live together or do not agree. In addition to the fathers having to reserve the right to parental leave benefits, but the right does not matter, without contact with the child.

In relation to father's leave, 3 models can be made. An extension of several months for the father so that everyone is happy, an earmarking of months of the current period, which is what will have the greatest effect in society or a transfer model where father and mother each have several months that they optionally can give to the other parent.

Most recently, the EU has decided on a minimum of 2 months for children and fathers across Europe as a right, but is that enough? Can we really justify that to children and citizens who need to be treated with respect for family life and on an equal footing?

One option is a compromise, where you extend the father's earmarked leave today from 14 days to 2 months of the parental period and give the parents an extra 1 month. Then the whole paternal leave debate is probably resolved for the benefit of the child, the parents, the companies, and society.

The following things should be noted:

48. The child is not entitled to the same leave with the father and the mother.

49. The child is not entitled to leave with the father but only the mother.

50. The father currently has 14 days of earmarked leave in Denmark, but both parents do not have e.g., 3 months of leave.

51. The family economy governs who takes leave in the family when it is not earmarked.

52. There are fewer fathers in Denmark than in the rest of the Nordic countries who take leave because it is not earmarked.

53. The execute order on parental leave gives the parent where the child stays most of the maternity benefit in case of disagreement, which means that the child and father are without rights in practice.

54. Fathers do not receive the same advice, support, and information during leave.

55. Fathers are not offered family groups in all municipalities.

56. Fathers are not offered to father's groups in all municipalities.

57. The child's attachment, security and psychological health with father and mother throughout life deteriorates.
58. The child's attachment, security, and psychological health e.g., in case of parental illness and death deteriorating.

59. There are fathers who do not want to take leave.

60. There are mothers who do not allow fathers to take leave.

61. There are employers who do not allow fathers to take leave when they are fired.

62. Many fathers do not know that they can take parental leave until the child reaches the age of 9.

63. The Parental Responsibility Act does not give the right to leave and visitation is required to take leave, which is not granted.

64. The Parental Responsibility Act discriminates against fathers in nuclear families and modern families in relation to leave.

65. Fathers often do not get time together for leave with small children due to the culture and women culture.

66. Fathers have no duty to take leave, only mother.

67. Mother's career opportunities are deteriorating.

68. Mother's pension deteriorates.

Theme 4: Child's residence

The most comprehensive and serious discrimination of children and fathers today is the division into residential and non-residential parents, when the parents do not live together.

It must be questioned regarding human rights whether such a division of ordinary children and parents is permitted in principle.

Ordinary children and parents experience division into residential and non-residential parents experience widely different legal, financial, and procedural rights. A clear direct and/or in-direct discrimination of citizens.

There is significant discrimination when the term is used as a starting point for families who live equally today. They suddenly must decide what status the parents should have just because they no longer live together. The concept must be considered as the most significant cause of family conflicts today at the end of cohabitation.

There is clear evidence of discrimination and gender discrimination. The number of children residing with fathers is still at the level of 1980 at the same time as there has been a marked development in the coexistence of children and fathers. The difference cannot be explained by the free choice of the families or the lack of desire of the fathers.

Fathers who want to, should and according to the law must have a residence for the children, simply do not get it, reality and statistics show.

The possibility of dual residence has recently been introduced based on the parents' mutual wish, but the address for the child must still be registered with one parent who only receives welfare benefits for the child.

At the same time, the family court and the courts cannot decide on dual residence, even if it is in the best interests of the child and create peace between equal parents. It is indirect gender discrimination. Neither direct nor indirect gender discrimination is permitted.

The following things should be noted:

69. Family law is historically built around one parent instead of the child and the whole family in a society that today lives equally. It is the foundation of the law that does not match today's society.

70. There is no free choice for your own agreement on the child's finances and visitation if the parents do not live together.

71. There is no free choice for school with both parents if the parents do not live together and there is not equal parenting time as the basic assumption.

72. There is no free choice of the child doctor if the parents do not live together.

73. There is no free choice of the child dentist if the parents do not live together.

74. There is no free choice for the child municipal activities for both parents if the parents do not live together.

75. The child does not have a passport with both parents if the parents do not live together.

76. Change of school can take place without the consent of both parents.

77. Change of after-school programs takes place without the consent of both parents.

78. Relocation of resident parents further away from the child's safe environment is allowed.

79. Relocation of residential parents further away from the child's school, peers and other parent is permitted, even though there is a 6-week notice period. There is no suspensive effect.

80. Participation of the child in children mental health groups require the acceptance of resident parents.

81. School psychologist for the child requires acceptance of residential parents.

82. The child are not treated equally when detained by the parents from visitation.

83. The child are not treated equally when the child is detained by the parents during holidays.

84. when the child is detained by the parents in high conflict cases, as the question of guilt does not apply.

85. Residential parents can threaten with less contact in disagreements about other things.

86. Children's residence with the father is still on a par with 1980 despite a positive father development in society.

87. The fathers have been given equal parenting time instead of residence or have been pushed out of the children's lives if they have complained.

88. The fathers experience extensively that children are "abducted" at the end of cohabitation and kept away to obtain residence and welfare benefits. However, it is only in foreign cases that there is legal recognition of abductions.

89. Children often do not get residence with fathers for historical and cultural reasons in the public sector.

90. Children often do not get residence with fathers when the child is small, even though there are fathers with 6-12 months of paternity leave who can easily handle the task.

91. Children often do not get residence with fathers when one parent tells untrue stories without consequences.

92. Children often do not get residence with fathers when the case is dragged out by parents or lawyers.

93. Children often do not get residence with fathers, even though they have had long leave and are the primary parent.

94. Children are not treated equally at their parents in cases of social history, mental illness, and negative social inheritance.

95. Children are not treated equally at their parents in cases of violence.

96. Children are not treated equally at their parents when the parents are violating the child.

97. Non-resident parents do not have to take responsibility for the child.

Theme 5: Children economics

If you are an EU citizen and work in Denmark, you are entitled to family allowance, whether you are married or divorced. This even if the child lives in another country.

National fathers/non-resident parents are however not entitled to the family allowance. This although they for example have equal parenting time and pay child support, hobbies, cell phone, clothe and other items. Not even if the fathers/non-resident parent become unemployed and have documented need for financial support in relation to the children.

In some cases, this may mean that the children lose contact with their father.

Today, the parents cannot distribute the child's parenting time and finances as they wish if they do not live together, e.g., if the mother needs the welfare benefits the most, but the child is best off for a shorter or longer period with the father. The address must be registered where the child stays the most and decide the distribution of the benefits.

The child's finances are to a large extent decisive for who is granted residence for the child, because only resident parents receive welfare benefits for the child. This must be considered as discrimination against citizens if a parent has a real need for welfare benefits.

The children economics form the basis for many family conflicts and for the child's parenting time arrangements, simply because only one parent can receive welfare benefits, family allowance and child support.

The distribution of the child's finances is experienced systematically as forming the basis for false accusations against fathers to a greater or lesser extent. This creates a negative social heritage for generations of children.

The following things should be noted:

98. The family allowances are sent out of the country, while fathers/non-resident parents receive nothing.

99. Parents must be registered as a resident and non-resident parent if they do not live together, which creates conflicts for equal parents, or when a parent wants the welfare benefits.

100. Child and youth benefit are paid to the mother.

101. Family allowance and child benefits is paid only to residential parents.

102. Housing benefits for children is paid only to resident parents.

103. Special child benefits for education seekers is paid only to resident parents.

104. Increased educational support for parents with children is paid only to resident parents.

105. Free cost in day care is allocated only to resident parents.

106. Disability benefits are granted to resident parents and do not always accompany the child.

107. Non-resident parents do not have the opportunity to get an au-pair.

108. A special supplement for the work of the municipal council is paid to resident parents.

109. Free trial for the child is granted only to resident parents.

110. Transport when moving further away is a joint responsibility, but there are no sanctions. It should be the responsibility of the moving parent as a basic assumption.

111. There is a fee for fathers in the hospitals at birth.

112. Child support is calculated solely on the income of the father/non-resident parents, even though the resident parent may be a millionaire and the non-resident parent unemployed.

113. Child support is calculated without considering the parents' ability to pay in the event of illness, unemployment, or fairness (e.g., eviction, harassment, or "abduction")

114. Child support is calculated so that there is no incentive for fathers/non-resident parents to create growth and increased earnings in society. The child support benefits the mother/resident parent and not necessarily the child.

115. Child support is granted despite the financial obligation for the child is fulfilled in 60/40 or 70/30 parenting time

arrangements without considering extra payments of hobbies, .travel, mobile phones etc.

116. Both parents must decide after-school program, but non-resident parents must pay full price, even though it may only be 1-5-day requirement if the resident parent does not want to pay.

117. Parents who do not live together but collaborates positively related to the child are discriminated compared to parents living as a traditional family

118. Fathers do not always want to pay child support and therefore want equal parenting arrangements.

119. Mothers sometimes want to receive child support and therefore do not want equal parenting arrangements

Theme 6: International parenting

Children and fathers are without equal rights in many countries for cultural and historical reasons.

The term "Ordre public", which is intended to protect legal certainty, has been attempted written out of the legislation or is not used.

If an authority do not use "Ordre public" and for example reject obviously unreasonable child support in the absence of rights for children of both parents or obviously unreasonable child support, where, for example, children are "kept away" from a parent despite court decisions, children and specially fathers are in a serious situation.

Many children have lost a healthy contact to especially fathers, who are financially ruined and destroyed as human beings without the help of the authorities.

Additionally, it is crucial for all children and parents that children are not allowed to move abroad automatically and without careful consideration of the human rights and law on children economics. It may be best for the child to stay in the country with the other parent.

Nordic families are further ahead than the rest of Europe and most parts of the world in terms of family law and equal family life. Such cultural differences and the upbringing location can have a great impact on the children.

Legal protection of children and parents should be provided on a better and more qualified basis based on the child's right to the father and the mother, as well as the cultural upbringing and location.

The following things should be noted:

120. In many countries, fathers are without rights due to outdated legislation, culture, and family law.

121. Fathers are not legally protected by "Ordre public" against obvious unreasonableness.

122. Fathers experience being without rights to enforce agreed parenting time.

123. Fathers must pay alimony for children abroad contrary to "Ordre public".

124. Fathers must pay parental leave support for children residing abroad in contravention of "Ordre public".

125. Fathers must pay child support for children abroad contrary to "Ordre public".

126. Fathers must pay court costs for children abroad contrary to "Ordre public".

127. Fathers must pay for residence and transport abroad contrary to "Ordre public".

128. Fathers must pay support for several years' contrary to "Ordre public".

129. Fathers can receive prison sentences abroad due to misinformation or inability to pay.

130. Fathers experience that children are kept away abroad to ensure the child's attachment and parent resident status.

131. Fathers experience that children travel abroad with their mother due to sole custody and stay e.g., with grandparents or with the mother abroad.

132. Fathers experience that children move with the mother abroad before forced placement.

133. Fathers experience that children are "abducted" by women's networks even though several cases have been stopped through the international Haager treaty cooperation.

134. Fathers experience beatings or they could be killed if they try to maintain contact with the child in certain countries.

135. Fathers experience having to pay child support even if the child has been abducted.

136. Parents experience that they must find and bring their abducted children home from abroad themselves.

137. Parents experience a lack of support in cases with children abroad.

138. Parents experience that they cannot afford to take cases about children abroad to court.

139. Parents get married in one country but divorced in another country without a different national law.

Theme 7: Public children cases

Doing the analysis for the gender equality catalog approximately 1.000 public children cases was gathered. The cases were divided into categories for further analysis following children in the public process.

The children process was analyzed related to time, quality, equality, flexibility, and costs. It was hereby relatively easy to see how often and where things went wrong for children and parents specially fathers in the public sector.

The process analysis showed there were far too many changes of hands between public entities and individuals, which resulted in loss of knowledge, process time and human error.

When the family law is too complex and outdated based on single parenting, where discrimination of children and parents in relation to family forms, the child's resident and gender happens every day, public employees often do not have the opportunity to do a proper job.

Also it was found that the family law was made in several ministries without coordination and the law was overlapping as well as being outdated. Policymakers in the ministries has no desire to admit this in public due to their careers and support of ministers from scandals.

This is a well-known management problem in complex human processes, which are termed predictable surprises. A management problem and responsibility that can be handled, but the will must be present and basic human rights respected.

The following things should be noted:

140. Children and parents experience extensive waiting times in the legal family system, which must be considered a violation of human rights. Children has the right to know and be cared for by their parents as well as the right for a fair trial within reasonable time applies for all citizens.

141. Fathers experience widespread gender discrimination in legislation and public practice.

142. Parents experience extensive discrimination in the same situation due to the use of resident and non-resident parents.

143. Fathers experience that gender is rewarded instead of behavior contrary to the best interests of the child.

144. Fathers experience being talked down by child experts in the family court system with underlying rules of thumb without an individual and concrete assessment.

145. Fathers experience being talked down to by child experts in the family court system without it being recorded in the minutes and appearing in the notes.

146. Fathers experience formal and informal cooperation between public authorities and private mother and child organizations.

147. Fathers experience formal and informal cooperation of a "monopoly" like nature with private mother and child organizations.

148. Fathers experience child advisors and child experts who do not disclose their background and experience.

149. Fathers experience child advisors who do not have a duty to take or journalize notes.

150. Fathers experience child advisors who are not subject to the right of access to documents from private individuals.

151. Fathers experience child advisors who do not comply with the Personal Data Act.

152. Fathers experience child advisors primarily are women.

153. Fathers experience child advisors who document conversations without regard to the Personal Data Act.

154. Fathers experience 3rd party child advisors without the authorities being able to document their "professionalism".

155. Fathers experience 3rd party child advisors where the authorities are unable to document their "child certificates".

156. Fathers most often experience that a child advisor is not the neutral offer to the child as it is presented as.

157. Fathers most often experience that they and the child are not entitled to a child advisor.

158. Fathers most often experience that child advisors are not transparent, which jeopardizes legal certainty.

159. Fathers most often experience that child advisors get involved after a stay with the mother.

160. Fathers most often experience that child meetings focus on the child's perspective in the short term.

161. Fathers most often experience that child meetings take place after a stay with the mother and the child are followed to the meeting by the mother.

162. Fathers often experience that child meetings are not always in the best interest of the child, as the child is caught in a loyalty conflict.

163. Fathers most often experience parental alienation, which harms the child throughout life.

164. Fathers most often experience parental alienation, which has no consequences.

165. Fathers most often experience parental alienation, which causes the child and father to lose contact.

166. Fathers most often experience serious consequences such as suicidal thoughts due to parental alienation and psychological violence.

167. Fathers most often experience that negative social heritage is repeated for generations due to parental alienation.

168. Fathers most often experience that parental alienation is not treated for the child.

169. Parents experience a lack of prevention of family cases.

170. Parents experience a lack of a positive free choice if they do not live together

171. Fathers experience a lack of equal mediation, counselling, and support.

172. Fathers experience that mediation cannot and should not take place without equal opportunities.

173. Parents experience that mediation should not take place in serious circumstances.

174. Parents experience long waiting times.

175. Parents experience long case processing.

176. Fathers most often experience that temporary change of resident is not happening, when the resident parent is moving away, wail the case is handled by the court.

177. Fathers most often experience subjective and undocumented assessments in children's cases in contrast to modern research on children's health in shared parenting.

178. Parents experience newly trained caseworkers in children's cases.

179. Fathers most often experience that personal relationships, e.g., own childhood and own divorce, have importance for professionals and decisions in the family system due to the mainly female workers.

180. Parents experience what is like friend favors at a management level.

181. Parents shall pay fees although they must start a child case.

182. Parents shall pay fees even if they win the case e.g., a clear reduction or increase in child support by law.

183. Fathers most often experience large legal costs in children's cases and may not be able to afford to pursue the case.

184. Parents experience too many people and authorities involved in children's cases.

185. Parents experience that basic rules of competence and ethics are not observed.

186. Parents can change agreements with fake signatures without it being discovered.

187. Parents experience that the municipality shall take care of the mother / resident parent and the Family Court system the father / non-resident parent, if the parents do not live together.

188. Fathers have a bad impression of the Family Court system due to gender discrimination.

189. Fathers have a bad impression of the Family Court system due to the gender distribution.

190. Fathers have a bad impression of the Family Court system due to discriminatory legislation.

191. Fathers have a bad impression of the Family Court system due to incorrect information being allowed.

192. Fathers have a bad impression of the Family Court system due to lack of experience by caseworkers, e.g., if they are not parent's themselves.

193. Fathers have a bad impression of the Family Court due to lack of consequence and reward of gender instead of behavior.

194. Fathers have a bad impression of the Family Court due to lack of recognition and correction of errors.

195. Fathers have a bad impression of the Family Court due to lack of information about the legislation's discrimination to ministries and policymakers.

196. Fathers give up complaining because they do not know how.

197. Fathers give up complaining because they give up.

198. Fathers give up complaining to protect their children.

199. Fathers give up complaining due to the processing time.

200. Fathers give up complaining due to the legal costs.

201. Fathers give up complaining due to discrimination as they know they will lose. The national gender equality and human right control institutions refers to the fact that the term resident and non-resident parent is the law and do not take human rights into consideration. Even though e.g., the number of children living with fathers is at the level of 1980 and significantly documents discrimination.

202. Fathers give up complaining because the complaint goes to the caseworker herself.

203. Fathers experience a lack of consideration for incapacity in children's cases.

204. Fathers experience that it easy for the mother to cheat the system.

205. Fathers experience a marked majority of female caseworkers and professionals approximately 90%

206. Fathers experience deficient information based on gender.

207. Fathers experience shorter speaking time based on gender.

208. Fathers experience less support based on gender.

209. Fathers experience that negative social heritage is repeated for generations due to gender discrimination.

210. Fathers experience false accusations based on gender.

211. Parents experience a lack of interdisciplinary cooperation in the public sector.

212. Parents experience a lack of continuity in the cases in relation to persons.

213. Parents experience that many different public institutions are involved with loss of knowledge between them.

214. Fathers experience inconsistency with false information and accusations.

215. Fathers experience that authorities problematize cases for the children for no reason.

216. Fathers experience that children threaten suicide or commit suicide due to mistreatment and gender discrimination.

217. Parents experience that negative social heritage is repeated for generations due to mistreatment.

218. Parents experience removal of children from the family, where the law has not been followed and support would probably work.

219. Parents experience removal of children from foreign citizens, where the embassy is not contacted.

220. Fathers feel that they have not been considered on removal of the children from the mother, because the child resident initially was given to the wrong parent.

221. Fathers often experience that it is not considered that the child's father can give the child the best upbringing.

222. Parents experience a lack of formal education and certification of pediatricians.

223. Parents experience that there are many persons and authorities in a case where a child is being removed from the family, whereby knowledge is lost, time is lost, and errors are not discovered or corrected.

224. Parents find that foster families sometimes do so for financial reasons.

225. Parents experience that foster families are sometimes not certified and quality approved well enough.

226. Parents experience that among professionals there is sometimes a wave of placements, as a kind of "fashion" phenomenon, also called the Chicago effect.

227. Parents experience that the family court system does not always act.

228. Parents experience that the family court system cannot always be contacted.

229. Parents experience that the family court does not always enforce contact-preserving contact.

230. Parents experience that the municipal does not always assist and facilitate in contact-preserving contact.

231. Parents experience that the family court decisions are not always based on the best cooperating parents.

232. The police do not check patterns of concern unless the victim himself will report.

233. The police are not involved in cases where parents document the untruths to the authorities.

234. False cases take sparse resources from real cases, which therefor is not handled correct.

235. Unacceptable behavior is not always handled because the victim tries to put it behind him and moved forward.

236. Unacceptable behavior is not always treated due to lack of evidence.

237. There are networks and lawyers who deliberately use misinformation as a method in child cases without consequence.

Theme 8: Violence against children & fathers

In relation to the violence effort, there are profoundly serious shortcomings in the knowledge, understanding and statistics of the authorities in Denmark.

There is an almost one-sided support for the efforts to combat violence against women. In addition, it is often women's organizations or women's projects without a prober interface with children and fathers or competencies that receive financial support.

It is often officially estimated that more women than men experience violence in family life. However, surveys by governmental children organizations and surveys with fathers illustrate that this is not correct in the Nordic countries today.

Neither public violence in the form of discrimination nor parental alienation, psychological and financial violence against fathers, is included, which is often what affects fathers in family life.

It is remarkable how the fathers first discover the discrimination at the end of cohabitation, and how the especially many equal fathers and children are not treated equally in the same situation.

In the area of violence, no prober support is provided in relation to the contact surface for children and fathers.

The father associations stand significantly with most of the abused children and fathers without receiving financial and governmental support like the women organizations. The investment for the prevention of violence in family life is often lost as a result.

It is often ordinary children and fathers who experience the violence, and the assessment is that today there may well be more men exposed to violence in family than women in the Nordic countries.

Violence is violence - and all victims, whether women, men, boys, or girls, must have the necessary support.

There are two conditions that are significant. The difference in funding is partly a problem for the children and fathers who are affected. The imbalance in funding also makes the statistics and understanding of gender-based violence misleading.

It is simply possible to support, collect statistics, hold meetings with politicians and make the victims visible when one receives massive state funding and has thousands of employees in the women's cause.

The seriousness is that the real victims are not being adequately and properly helped, in addition to creating mistrust and disrespect for the violence when it takes place unilaterally against reality and in dense old networks.

The following things should be noted:

238. Fathers are not always informed that they are to be fathers.

239. Fathers do not always get their name on the birth certificate, as a surname or middle name.

240. Fathers are not always allowed to take parental leave.

241. Fathers are not always allowed to attend baptisms.

242. Fathers experiences they have been abused to be fathers.

243. Fathers become unvoluntary fathers after few hours of contact, despite contraception being the responsibility of both parents. They can be misled even in marriages.

244. Fathers experience that they do not receive help when they get postpartum depressions.

245. Fathers experience that the negative social heritage of the other parent shows up at the time of birth.

246. Fathers experience no help when mothers have a postpartum depression, and the father lose contact with their child.

247. Fathers experience that they cannot get double residence because the mother does not want to without prober reason.

248. Fathers experience that they do not get the child's residence because the mother wants the child's welfare benefits.

249. Fathers experience that they do not get the child's residence because the authorities believe the mother needs the child's welfare benefits.

250. Fathers experience that they do not get equal or the parenting time that is best for the child, because the mother wants the child's welfare benefits.

251. Official governmental institutions today find that children experience lighter violence from the mother more than the father.

252. Official governmental institutions today find that child experience more psychological violence from the mother than the father.

253. Official governmental institutions today find that children experience the same harsh violence from their father and mother.

254. Fathers most often experience that the child is removed upon termination of cohabitation and kept away from them for no objective reason.

255. Fathers experience being exposed to parental alienation.

256. Fathers most often experience being exposed to misinformation and false accusations because the mother wants the child's residence and the most time with the child.

257. Fathers experience not getting equal parenting time because some mothers think that the child is always better off with the mother.

258. Fathers experience financial extortion, e.g., pay an amount in the mailbox or buy a dress or shoes to get parenting time.

259. Fathers experience that they are exposed to light or harsh physical violence but does not receive help.

260. Fathers experience that they are exposed to psychological violence but does not receive help.

261. Fathers experience that they are exposed to psychological violence and can be told it is not their child after all.

262. Fathers experience that they are exposed to psychological violence by being told late in life that they have a child.

263. Fathers experience that they are exposed to financial violence by both working and doing most domestic work.

264. Fathers experience false accusations that they suddenly are not good enough as parents when legal decisions are to be made.

265. Fathers experience false accusations that the child does not thrive e.g., in visitation cases when legal decisions are to be made.

266. Father experience false accusations of violence without consequences.

267. Fathers experience false accusations of sexual assault without consequences.

268. Fathers experience parental alienation without consequences.

269. Fathers experience lack of offers for counselling and support when they are abused.

270. Fathers experience large dark numbers in relation to the statistics on violence against children and fathers.

271. Fathers experience accusations of" victim mentality" if they state that they have been subjected to violence.

272. Fathers experience violence that they cannot report, as this raises the level of conflict, and it will often harm the father and child contact, as the question of guilt is not valid due to discrimination.

273. Fathers experience a marked imbalance in public funding to support violence against men and women.

274. Fathers experience that the effort against violence is incorrectly financed in relation to contact surfaces and needs.

275. Fathers are not treated equally on housing offers and crisis centers in connection with termination of cohabitation and / or violence.

276. Fathers do not, as mothers do, receive free psychological assistance.

277. Fathers can as well be violent towards women, but fathers experience marked discrimination when it happens to them.

278. Mothers may experience many of the same things and in some cases other types of violence than fathers, but they do not experience the same imbalance in the recognition, support, statistical collection, and funding of family violence.

279. Parents, regardless of gender, experience violence in close relationships suddenly at the end of cohabitation.

280. Parents experience false accusations of abuse and neglect.

281. Parents experience false reports to the municipality without reason or consequence.

282. Parents discover that errors related to public children cases are not detected, acknowledged, or corrected.

283. Fathers most often experience that the question of guilt does not matter and that it harms the child.

284. Fathers most often experience that decisions are based on the subjective and undocumented assessments of caseworkers.

285. Fathers, like mothers, experience that the child is exposed to light and or severe violence by another parent.

286. Fathers, like mothers, experience that another parent becomes violent due to alcohol.

287. Fathers experience, like mothers, that another parent becomes violent due to birth reactions.

288. Fathers, like mothers, experience that another parent, both with and without psychiatric medication, becomes violent.

289. Fathers, like mothers, experience that another parent becomes violent due to stress in everyday life.

290. Fathers, like mothers, experience that another parent becomes violent due to negative social inheritance.

291. Fathers experience systematic hate speech and harassment by mothers, mother' networks, and extreme women groups.

292. Fathers experience systematic stalking by mothers, mother' networks and extreme women groups.

293. Fathers experience systematic child abductions by mothers, mother' networks and extreme women groups.

294. Fathers experience a widespread abuse of power by women in children and gender equality work.

Theme 9: Father responsibility

Based on interviews of women in relation to the father role and analysis of principled family cases for mothers, including placement cases and cases of violence, several patterns have been experienced related to fathers.

The following things should be noted:

295. Fathers should take equal responsibility for the children, if they are allowed, the parents agree, or the mother needs help.

296. Fathers should recognize biological parenthood.

297. Fathers should read public information about the child, if they receive it

298. Fathers should take more leave, if they are allowed.

299. Fathers should refrain from opting out of contact with their children, as this is of great importance for the children's self-esteem later in life.

300. Fathers should spend time with their children instead of just, work, sports, or friends.

301. Fathers should attend school and general meetings and activities about the children.

302. Fathers should refrain from requiring equal parenting time to avoid child support.

303. Fathers should understand that physical, mental, economic, or sexual violence is never acceptable.

304. Fathers should distance themselves from sexual and gender-based harassment.

305. Fathers should take leave so that mother has better job opportunities e.g., after graduation.

306. Fathers should take leave so that the mother's career opportunities become equal, if desired

307. Fathers shall be aware that both parents experience many of the same things and feelings related to the child if they are stay-at-home parents or have longer parental leave.

Theme 10: Lawyer's methods & ethics

It is well known that lawyers act gender-based in legal family cases due to the gender discrimination in law and practices. It is easy to cheat the system when rewarding happens based on gender instead of behavior.

In bar associations and family lawyers' associations knowing this in general has not made any effort to secure that matter. That in relation to the patterns in lawyers' ethics and methods in family court cases with children in the middle.

Bar associations can introduce a whistleblower scheme, which is a good start, but these are conditions that cannot be excused by family lawyers. It is clearly not in the best interest of the child, nor is children and fathers experiencing a fair trial according to the human rights conventions.

The following things should be noted:

308. Fathers experience that family lawyers and the legal community continue to ignore the obvious gender discrimination that takes place in family law.

309. Fathers experience that lawyers behave markedly differently in relation to clients' gender in family cases due to gender discrimination in legislation and practice. It happens without consequences.

310. Fathers experience that lawyers often pull the parents apart with children in the middle.

311. Fathers experience that lawyers deliberately raise the level of conflict for mothers due to gender discrimination.

312. Mothers experience that lawyers deliberately reduce the level of conflict for fathers due to gender discrimination.

313. Fathers experience that lawyers do not admit and change mistakes although they have documentation.

314. Fathers experience that lawyers want the case brought to court to obtain higher fees or free trial for clients paid by the state.

315. Fathers experience that lawyers provide the family court system with incorrect information about the child directly or indirectly against better judgement.

316. Fathers experience that lawyers cover up violence by mothers by attacking the father.

317. Fathers experience that lawyers indirectly recommend mothers to make false accusations.

318. Fathers experience that the legal community to date has done virtually nothing in relation to the problem.

319. Fathers experience that family lawyers ignore the problem of lawyers' ethics and methods.

320. Fathers experience that lawyers refer perpetrators to shelters for no objective reason to have a stronger case.

321. Fathers experience that lawyers systematically escalate conflicts for the benefit of the mother.

322. Fathers experience that attorneys systematically drag cases out to prolong the best interests of their client.

323. Fathers experience that lawyers systematically drag cases out for long periods of time for financial pressure.

324. Fathers most often find that lawyers scale their wealth against better judgement for the benefit of the mother.

325. Fathers experience that the same lawyer names reoccur in cases of gross false allegations for decades.

Theme 11: Funding, statistics & research

In Denmark alone the State Audit has found approx. 5.8 billion DKK per year in social funds, of which approx. 50% of the pools were so-called "secret" pools that is regarded illegal. This has happened for decades.

As a result of the investigation, it was also found in Denmark alone that a senior official illegally took more than 100 mill. DKK over a period of 20 years. Just as another example of unreasonable and incorrect allocations of state funds going to a large degree to women and women organizations.

There is still even today a lacking explanation by ministers and ministries of how this could happen and who is responsible. Who have received this money every year on what basis, by whom and for what? What has been the consequences for children and fathers in society?

Political votes are a good indication of the cause of these legal conflicts with human rights, legal standards and gender equality in the country stated to have the least corruption in the world.

If one compares the public revenues in the annual accounts of the largest mother and child organizations with the largest father and child organizations, there is profound gender discrimination in the state funding.

The ministries and politicians do not respond objectively and adequately to the problem or the human rights issues, including the significance of a skewed allocation for children's equal contact with father and mother in life.

There is a marked lack of interest in taking responsibility for the gender discrimination that has occurred for decades in state funding and continues to occur for children and fathers in the public sector.

It is further documented through analyzes that official family research has often been based on mother and child answers, as the questionnaires have not been sent to the fathers.

The statistics that are made in the family area are to a large extent culturally influenced by the women movement's desire for gender equality. There are often clear and obvious signs that project support, statistics and research are made by women for women with women.

This is, of course, a serious problem in relation to equality and respect of human rights, which applies for all citizens.

The following things should be noted:

326. The State Audit has in Denmark alone found DKK 5.8 billion per year in social funds, of which approx. 50% was awarded in "secret funds" regarded illegal.

327. The ministries have still not explained adequately what has happened and how the allocations have been made.

328. The ministries have still not explained who has received the many billions every year in secret funds.

329. The ministries have still not held officials and politicians accountable for the many billions in "secret funds."

330. The ministries have not held officials accountable for the obvious lack of control.

331. The ministries do not recognize gender discrimination and discrimination against citizens. They do not even want to talk about it.

332. The ministries appear to have no interest in acknowledging and telling politicians about their own mistakes in law.

333. There are no statistics on single or shared custody for all children under 18 years of age.

334. There are no statistics on visitation arrangements for all children under 18 years of age.

335. The number of children residing with fathers is still at the level of 1980, contrary to societal developments.

336. Statistics on violence against men are grossly deficient and do not consider public violence (discrimination), parental alienation and psychological violence, which are the most prevalent.

337. No emphasis is placed on contact surfaces for children and fathers in application evaluations for social funds.

338. No emphasis is placed on preventive action against children and fathers in application evaluations for social funds.

339. There is no equal treatment of applicants from a qualitative perspective between women and men.

340. No state funds are provided for children and father organizations compared with children and mother organizations.

341. No state funds are provided for father organizations with unsubstantiated explanations of applications.

342. No state funds are provided for father organizations, despite markedly largest contact surface for fathers exposed to violence.

343. State funds are given unilaterally to women councils with markedly skewed gender distribution.

344. There is a lack of training of employees who must allocate state funds in relation to equality, human rights and children and fathers.

345. The allocation of state funds is based on old networks and is not experienced objective for children and citizen needs.

346. National family research used for law changes has been documented to be based on mother answers alone.

347. National family research used for law changes has been documented to be based on female answers found in researchers' own networks.

348. National family research used for law changes has been based on researchers and expert groups with 90% - 100% women participants.

349. National family research used for law changes has a blind spot in relation to children and fathers as well as shared parenting – and the positive benefits of this for society.

Theme 12: How can it happen?

The Gender Equality Catalog raises serious questions about ministerial leadership and respect of human rights.

There is a total lack of recognition, accountability, respect for human rights, adequate orientation of politicians and learning in the public sector.

In addition, "gatekeeping" at various levels in what at times resembles the monopoly and cartel formation of the women's cause in the child and gender equality efforts and family legislation against the best interests of the child and society.

Why has nothing happened to children and fathers? and how can this be allowed to happen?

It is often women who experience abuse of power in work life and men who experience abuse of power in family life. The many women in the field of children and gender equality often talk about themselves and their own. Is this not abuse of power?

The following things should be noted:

350. Where has the national governments been for children and fathers?

351. Where has the national ministries for children, gender equality and social affairs been for children and fathers?

352. Where has the official equality control boards been for children and fathers?

353. Where has the Human Rights Institutions been for children and fathers?

354. Where has national research institutions been for children and fathers?

355. Where has national gender equality institutions been for children and fathers?

356. Where has the national children's council been for children and fathers?

357. Where has the family courthouse been for children and fathers?

358. Where has the family courts been for children and fathers?

359. Where has the ombudsman been for children and fathers?

360. Where has the 100% women board of the national family law association been for children and fathers?

361. Where is the European Commission been for children and fathers?

362. Where is the United National 'Woman' Committee on Gender Equality been for Children and Fathers?

363. Where is United Nations Nordic 'Woman' Committee on Gender Equality been for children and fathers?

364. Where are the United Nations and world goals for children and fathers?

365. Where are the national parliaments for children and fathers?

366. Where are the responsible officials who must comply with and inform politicians about human rights for children and fathers?

It is remarkable how information and the need for equality of children and fathers simply do not come up through the national governmental and institutional human rights system. The problem is ignored or kept down.

It is about will, lobbying, culture and change. The experience and documentation of discrimination against children and fathers is significant.

In the same way that we experienced boards only with men decades ago, the challenge today 100 years of women's culture within gender equality.

It is largely only women who participate in the gender equality work, which of course has shaped, and every day shapes the legislation and practices in society.

It is well documented and can be said in one word what happens to children and fathers.

Gender discrimination

Nordic benchmark

The Nordic countries has been compared in consultation with experienced children and father organizations and there are only few differences. It is the same patterns we see in the Nordic countries and in most of Europe.

Themes	DK	SE	NO	IS	FI
Parenthood	2	2	2	2	1
Public information	3	3	2	3	4
Paternal leave	2	5	4	5	2
Living residence	3	2	2	1	2
Ligeværdig tid	2	4	2	4	4
Children economics	2	2	2	2	1
Public children cases	3	1	1	1	1
International parenting	3	2	1	2	2
Violence onchildren and fathers	2	1	1	1	1
Funding and research	2	3	2	2	2
Average	2,4	2,5	1,9	2,3	2,0

Level 5: Gender equality
Level 4: Reform implementation
Level 3: Political reform decision
Level 2: Political reform preparation
Level 1: Reforms not started

There is every reason to take the situation seriously. It could be here we find the one of the important reasons for lack of respect for equality as well as children's mental health problems, social spending, and instability in society.

For most children, the love and care by the father and mother are the most important thing in life. For most parents, children are the most important thing in life.

It often leaves deep scars in the soul if there is not a good and loving upbringing and contact between children and parents.

We can do better as society!

Thank you for important insights and contributions to these Nordic children and father organizations:

Denmark: Foreningen Far
www.foreningenfar.dk

Norway: Mannsforum
www.mannsforum.no

Sweden: VBU
www.vbu-se.se

Iceland: Foreldrajafnretti
www.foreldrajafnretti.is

Finland: Lasten Oikeudet
www.lastenoikeudet.fi/